To my bunch. You guys are my world.
I will love you all, always.

Text and Illustrations © 2014 Kim Kho Riley

Kilmac Press Books
Visit us on the Web! www.kilmacpressbooks.com

ISBN 978-0-9907059-0-1 (paperback)
ISBN 978-0-9907059-0-8 (hardcover)
ISBN 978-0-9907059-2-5 (E-Book)

Bubbs

Kim Kho Riley

Illustrated by Mentol Art

I have a baby brother.
I call him Bubbs.
He has bubbly cheeks.

Bubbs has brown hair.

So do I.

Bubbs likes green beans.

So do I.

Bubbs likes carrots.

I don't like carrots.

Bubbs is my half-brother.
That sounds silly to me.

How can Bubbs be
half a brother?

When I have half a cookie, it is just as yummy as a whole cookie.

When I have half a sandwich, it still goes straight to my tummy.

Bubbs' dad is Steve.
My dad is Steve, too.

We have the same Dad.

Bubbs' mom is Kate.   My mom is Ann.

We have different moms.
We look a little different, too.

Bubbs and I have a lot of fun.
He calls me Charlie.
I love being a big brother.

When Bubbs was born, I gave him a teddy bear.

It was just like the one Dad gave me when I was a baby.

We named him Toby.

One day, we visited Grandpa Sam
and his little dog, Oscar.

Bubbs and I love visiting
Grandpa Sam and Oscar.

We had fun until...Oscar bit Toby.

Toby was broken in half.

Bubbs was very, very sad.

I had a great idea to help Bubbs.
I asked my step-mom, Kate, to sew
Toby back together again.

Bubbs was so happy to see Toby fixed.

Toby was a little different but
Bubbs loved him just the same.

Bubbs is my half-brother,
that makes us a little different, too.

But brothers are brothers,
and we love each other
just the same.

www.ingramcontent.com/pod-product-compliance
Lightning Source LLC
Chambersburg PA
CBHW040023050426
42452CB00002B/104